"Not since Louis Evely's *That M[...] book so delightfully powerful...[...] as well as inspiration.

"For the perplexed Catholic who wonders what has happened to the faith that was learned in grade school; for the 'cafeteria Catholic' who since Vatican II has picked up bits of renewed Catholicism and would like to see how it fits into the bigger picture; for the serious student of contemporary theology who struggles with the 'big names' and wants to meditate on the marvels of it all; and for those who long for theology in the key of C—here is a book to read and re-read and then hand on to someone else. It's that kind of book."

Fr. Edmond Dunn
St. Ambrose University

"Bill Huebsch has written one of the few books I didn't want to end. It isn't easy to write about grace, nor is it very exciting to read about it, but with his style, turn-of-phrase, and sensitivity to the human condition, Huebsch helps us experience grace as we read his reflections. His context is contemporary living, his scriptural insights are creative, his suggestions to experience grace (the Holy pause) are concrete and do-able ('holy sharing'), and his humor regularly rises to make the book all the more enjoyable."

Michael H. Crosby, OFMCap
Author of *Spirituality of the Beatitudes*

"Huebsch has looked with the eyes of faith through the lens of Scripture and has simply and movingly described what he sees: grace living and active in every aspect of our 'ordinary' experience. He not only contemplates God's presence in human life, but shows us how to do it for ourselves."

Bernard J. Bush, SJ
Grace Institute

BILL HUEBSCH

grace

GOD'S
GREATEST
GIFT

TWENTY THIRD 23rd
PUBLICATIONS
www.23rdpublications.com

TWENTY-THIRD PUBLICATIONS
A Division of Bayard
One Montauk Avenue, Suite 200
New London, CT 06320
(860) 437-3012 or (800) 321-0411
www.23rdpublications.com

ISBN 978-1-58595-783-5
Library of Congress Catalog Card Number: 2009937865
Printed in the U.S.A.

CONTENTS

INTRODUCTION

In the spring of 1981, I was a graduate student at Catholic Theological Union in Chicago's Hyde Park. I had found at CTU a community of students and teachers devoted to exploring the great questions of truth which people everywhere have explored for centuries.

Early in my time at CTU, I fell under the influence of Rev. Gene LaVerdière and I began to probe the Scriptures deeply. The question that I brought to my work with Scripture is the very one that I am undertaking here. As I heard Gene LaVerdière work with the text, I knew that I had found my teacher.

There were other courses and other teachers as well who patiently stood by as I rediscovered much that had gone before me in coming to understand how it is that Jesus brings people to wholeness, to grace.

But in the spring of 1981, I was enrolled in a seminar studying Karl Rahner's theology. The professor's name was Peter Schineller, a Jesuit.

I could never forget what we did there that spring. Only about fifteen of us had enrolled in the seminar and we spent the entire time together reading one book: Rahner's

Foundations. We read and struggled with this text, guided by Peter and several secondary sources.

As the semester slowly progressed, the excitement of the class began to grow because we were discovering a marvelous theology, systematic and faithful! It was hard work to uncover in English what this great scholar had written in German. (Even in German, scholars sometimes struggled to understand him.) He was presenting the nature of human existence as oriented toward a loving God. The hearer of the Word and the nature of the absolute mystery we encounter—all spellbinding to learn.

And then we came to chapter four. Simply titled, "The Event of God's Self-Communication," we as a group gradually discovered something powerful and moving. We peeled back layer after layer, as one might unwrap an onion, until we could see, dimly at first but more clearly as we progressed, what it means to receive grace as a free gift from a loving God, God's very own self-communication to us. The gift being given to us is received within our own very lives, our being. We become the event which is God's self-communication. This frees us to respond to God, but it also offers us forgiveness and healing. It offers us, in sum, a *relationship* with God. And this grace is offered to *everyone.*

It was as though the veil lifted slowly and we began to see clearly what that theology had been which stood behind the work done at Vatican II. We began to uncover what that understanding of grace had been which empowered the liturgical reformers, the formation movements of women religious, and the landmark work of the Scripture scholars earlier in this century. Here it was: *grace.*

We realized that the hard work we were doing, to pore over Rahner paragraph by paragraph, would yield rich results. But it was very hard work and that course overshadowed everything else I did that term in school.

However, while what Rahner had to say was wonderful; coming to understand it was not.

"God himself," Rahner wrote for example in *Foundations* (p. 137), "as the abiding and holy mystery, as the incomprehensible ground of man's [sic] transcendent existence is not only the God of infinite distance, but also wants to be the God of absolute closeness in a true self-communication, and he is present in this way in the spiritual depths of our existence as well as in the concreteness of our corporeal history."

This is exciting stuff. But what does it mean?

That's the present question; the central purpose of this book is to lay it out in plain English. Theology must be common; it cannot remain hidden in heavy-duty theological jargon. I remember thinking during that seminar that if everyone who has left the church could read and understand this, and if everyone who has remained would interiorize it, the scales would fall from our eyes and we would see the energy of the resurrection of Christ standing tall before us, empowering not only the church, but the world.

There is a great danger in what I am doing here. This presentation of grace is almost entirely without nuance and there is the danger that, because of that, it may be misunderstood. But I think we must take this risk. In a sense, as a valuable theological reflection, this is a "discussion draft." I hope that you will argue with me—and with others—about this. Have I sometimes gone too far to be inclusive? Have I sometimes not gone far enough? Is it too harsh in places? too psychologized? too simple? or still too complex?

If what we understand about God in our lives and our world is not debated among all the people, then we risk losing the value of human experience which is where, Rahner helps us to see, God can most readily be found.

■ THE TITLE ■

There have been many trends in psychology since Freud first made his observations in the late nineteenth century. Most of these trends are reported in books that have lined the shelves of shopping mall bookstores since the early 1970s. For the most part, I do not trust those trends but they are useful inasmuch as they are part of the whole discussion which is slowly uncovering the human mind.

However, I suspect that at least one of those popular movements is not a trend but a lasting dimension of all human healing: the wholeness movement. The healing of the whole person: mind, body, spirit, and soul, is as old as the Hebrew and Christian Scriptures and common to religious understanding from East to West.

These reflections rise out of that rich history of healing and are a spirituality of wholeness. They seek to provide a basis for our belief that God wants us to be whole and that God's grace can empower us for that.

.

1

Grace
IS REAL

Grace is a free gift from a loving God.
It's offered to everyone.
But it's hard to believe that.

The human being, explains Fr. Karl Rahner, SJ, is "the event of God's absolute and forgiving self-communication" (*Foundations of the Christian Faith: An Introduction to the Idea of Christianity*, trans by William V. Dych [New York: Seabury, 1978], pp. 116-137). God has, in a word, donated God's own very self to the world, in Creation and in Christ. This is grace for us, that God, all along and everywhere, has been giving God's own very life away to us human beings, in a generous, unending, enormous gift. This transforms our human knowing, our loving, our own very being.

Most of us learned about grace when we were children in religion class with a pastor or teacher. In those "good old days" we felt quite sure about grace and God and sin and all those things, which we knew we either had to seek or to avoid, in order to gain either heaven or hell. But today we're not as sure about religious matters, and to some extent, we've forgotten about this matter called grace.

We may have thought at one time that we could learn answers to all of life's most complex questions. We may have sought answers to questions that dealt with all the great mysteries of the church, answers that laid them out in a nice orderly fashion, like pairs of shoes in a closet. We may have had the idea that we could fully understand, and therefore, control the path of life.

We forgot in this seeking, that life is filled with mystery.

Grace is one of those mysteries, one that we yearned to know and understand. But the tricky thing about grace was that, even if we felt a sense of great spiritual certainty, we were still never quite sure, not quite absolutely sure, when we had it. But we were very sure when we didn't! The rules about losing grace seemed much clearer than the ways of obtaining grace.

One of the very important questions that religious seekers have on their minds often is: "Am I in the state of grace?" This is important. If one was not in the state of grace, we were once taught, and one were to suddenly die, one would go straight to hell. This seems rather harsh to us now, but for many Christians, it was considered a fact of life—and death. My own mother warned often of the dangers of eating meat on a Friday, for example. She worried that, after the high school ball game on a Friday night we might stop with our meat-eating friends at the Eagle Café in our home town and there, in a moment of weakness, we might order a burger and fries. If we did so of our own free will, knowing it was wrong, and intending to eat it, we committed a sin so serious that all grace was removed from our souls. If we were to die in a car crash on the way home that night, we would not see God in Heaven. Oh my.

I actually thought to myself many times that to show up in Hell for eternity having gotten there by eating meat on a Friday, would be a sorry lot for a sinner. I'd spend eternity being mocked by the really big sinners. "How did you get here?" they'd taunt. "Meatloaf" would be my pitiful answer. I'd be the laughingstock of Hell.

But this was never a joking matter. We did also know that we could, if we had the time as the car was crashing, make a perfect act of contrition which would temporarily restore us to the state of grace, but only until we could make a good confession. Still, it might get us as far as Purgatory.

Being outside the state of grace was a rather public condition for us because, when everyone else got up to go to communion during Mass, everyone in the church knew who was not in the state of grace, because they couldn't go. They had to sit there marked as the dirty sinners they were while all the lines filed past on their way to the communion rail. I used to wonder if people could guess why I didn't go to communion sometimes: "Do they know that I allowed an impure thought to linger longer than I should have?"

Certain terrible sins, as I just pointed out, could remove all grace from our souls. Certain actions or desires, even certain thoughts, could render us unfit for the Kingdom of God, and unpleasing enough to God so that we would be sealed in our perdition for eternity.

But God, we were assured, would only send us to hell if we insisted on it.

There wasn't much discrimination here: priests, nuns, bishops, lay people—all were fated alike when it came to "losing grace." And the sin that did it could be anything from eating that hamburger on a Friday to murder—both were equally "mortal sins." It could be anything from that "impure" thought allowed to linger for a moment to adultery and fornication. There was no sliding scale when it came to these things, at least not as many Christians were taught about them.

Now, if you were ever in doubt about what it took to lose grace, there was always someone nearby to ask: your pastor. The Pastor pretty much always knew. The point here is that in those days there were answers in the first place. We knew what was what and we knew that the "official" church would tell us.

And from certain sins the pastor could even give a dispensation. You could actually get permission in advance to go ahead and "commit the sin" but the punishment, the loss of grace, the threat of eternal damnation would be removed by the nod of the pastor's head.

It was a marvelous system for understanding and controlling the flow of grace. But it didn't stop here. It was also possible to store up grace and to earn it for others.

Storing up grace was always said to be a good idea. That way, if you died unexpectedly or if you accidentally committed a sin without really realizing it or if you just came up "short" on grace for some reason, you would have a little in your "account." You could earn grace, sort of like earning your allowance, by doing good works, by saying your prayers, by using certain blessed objects, by receiving certain blessings, by giving good example, by certain kinds of financial gifts, and in a whole variety of other ways. Apparently, though, you could not get it just by asking for it.

Earning grace and storing it up was the business of the spiritual life. It was the preoccupation of those seeking to be close to God. It was the primary focus of effort and the only way to heaven.

The trouble was that it took only one of those nasty mortal sins to undo all your earnings. One slip and your bank account was closed. If you spent your whole life trying to be good but slipped at the last minute, mercy was lost and you were doomed.

Earning grace for others was simpler and it was usually done after they'd died. It was a way to "earn" their way out of Purgatory and into Heaven.

▪ A NEW DAY ▪

At the Second Vatican Council, and in the theology being developed within the church prior and subsequent to that Council, we have returned to an earlier understanding of grace and mercy. The theology and practice of the church have advanced in the past fifty years. The trouble is that few of us adults have studied our faith for a very long time. Most of us depend on what we learned when we were children, even though it no longer serves us very well.

Many church members, for example, have committed certain serious sins which they failed to confess and they have gone on in their lives and hope to continue going on. But they believe the sins are there, on their souls or somewhere, and they aren't really sure what to do about that. They aren't even sure they were sins to begin with, but the doubts linger. They beg for attention, they search for answers.

Many Christians have just decided to ignore some of those childhood lessons in "religion" and to live with as much heart and goodness as they can muster. Many are tormented though. Some are afraid of God. Some still count sins as they do their shoes. Some are in doubt. Some don't know what to think anymore, and many have simply left the church because it was easier to do that than to unravel all those complicated sins and indulgences.

Many people prefer to take the risk that God will be merciful in the end rather than struggle with a system that no longer seems to meet their needs.

There is confusion in the church today about all of this. The confusion would be tolerable except that many people's lives are being lived in the shadow of a historical albatross over which they had no control but which now threatens to control them.

So we need to look at all of this again. We need to re-examine grace and re-ask those questions we once memorized. We need to talk together again because, while the truth about grace has not changed, the language we use to describe that truth has changed a great deal.

The language I learned as a child, the language our parents learned and dozens of generations before them, was a language of the twelfth century later frozen in time by anxious bishops at the Council of Trent, bishops fearful that without certainty, all the known world would unravel.

But today, because of the grace of Vatican II, we have a fresh language, a language of life and vitality, a language that promises to help those who take it seriously to move into the Heart of the Lord and the Heart of the Gospel. The trouble with today's new expression of these ancient truths is that it is written in heavy-duty theological language, a language that I'm convinced not even all the theologians always understand. We need to learn to talk about these things in plain, simple, everyday words, words that we understand. We take a risk in doing this that we will miss some of the nuances, some of the fine points, some of the minor distinctions, of the greater theological argument.

We are concerned with getting on with our spiritual lives and finding some guidance in the fresh and exciting ways of talking about these things that we have available today.

2

Grace
IS MYSTERIOUS

Life is filled with mystery.
It is not a mystery caused by confusion.
It is the divine mystery whose depths
we cannot plumb entirely.

Grace is perhaps the most important aspect of our faith. Part of the evidence is that it has been the theology of grace over which church leaders have disagreed for centuries: Is the grace of God sufficient that we are saved by faith alone? Or is grace such that, in order to obtain it, we must also perform good works in order to be saved?

Does grace have the power to change us interiorly, permanently, or essentially? Or does it merely cover over our sinful natures, which remain sinful, despite the presence of grace? Is grace something given freely by God to all? Or is it meted only to those who fulfill certain prescriptions of the law? Is it really possible for a person to lose grace completely? How could a person who has lost grace go on living?

Most people wouldn't know what to say if someone wanted them to define grace. Most people, if they thought about it much, would appear not to be affected on a day-to-day basis by grace, whatever it is. Most people, if push came to shove, would take their chances with the mercy of God rather than relying on what they perceive to be arcane theology. Most people, if it stood right before them, wouldn't have the faintest idea what grace even is or what it means to experience it or even what it all has to do with their faith.

Grace eludes our grasp and our understanding and our academic probing and pursuit. It is radically present in our lives, yet it cannot be touched or even seen. And the minute we try to capture grace, to corner the market on it, it seems to disappear into thin air. No explanation is sufficient.

In this way, grace is just like being human. Who could adequately define what that means? We could give a scientific explanation, defining the cells and impulses of the body, or we could even make a beginning in understanding the brain. But who can define the Mind? Who can explain the Human Spirit? Who could describe Personality? Who can touch the Soul?

Human beings, us: We stand constantly at the very edge of mystery. Our whole lives open into a kind of endlessness, a horizon reaching beyond our sight. We are always reaching another threshold on that horizon, yet we never reach the end of human potential. We jump farther, run faster, discover more, probe farther into space, and every year find yet another horizon.

It is as though we stand on the edge of a great primeval forest looking out across a great, unexplored, sunlit savannah: Dare we venture out into that unknown? Dare we not?

But as we stand on the edge of that mystery, the edge of that endless horizon of discovery, of energy, of love and laughter, we do not stand there alone. Deep within our spirit, buried in our bones, kept as a secret in our hearts, is a greater mystery yet, an energetic mystery that both draws us toward it and is the source of our power to proceed. We don't know much about this other mysterious force except that it seems sure to be there.

▦ THE STRENGTH WE NEED ▦

We have all experienced this: We come along in our lives day in and day out, until we come to something that we simply cannot explain: death, illness, beauty, love, birth, friendship, well-being, or whatever. At those times, we find ourselves moving forward, empowered by an energy that we do not understand and moving toward a new personal space, a new freedom, a new self-knowledge, a new strength, a new and greater depth. We say that we don't know where we ever got the strength and that is correct: This source of strength and this new growth both exceed our grasp.

If we are reflective we know it is present but we really do not know much else about it. It is ultimately beyond our comprehension.

But we take a certain comfort in knowing that this mysterious force is there. So we call on this mysterious energy for healing, peace, and love, and we name it: God. "God," we should remember, is our name for it, not its name for itself.

This experience of mystery is something that everyone has: It is not limited to Christians and certainly not to Catholics. It can form a deep bond of human solidarity; draw us together into one; bind us tightly to one another.

There is not very much that we can say with certainty about this Holy Mystery. But despite that, we have been talking about it through the ages. We have even fought wars about it, of all things!

In the end, we have only our human experience of mystery to go on. That may not seem like much, but when we collect our experiences together: write them down, tell stories about them, celebrate them, and reflect about them, we find that there is more there than we thought. But even when we study it and establish schools of theology to explore it deeply, we find that the mystery eludes us.

After all of this, we find that our best bet is simply to loosen our grip, lighten up, and let mystery be Mystery. When we stand back and let that happen, we find this Mystery gently revealing us to ourselves. We discover an inborn hunger for intimacy with Holy Mystery. And we experience in it deep acceptance, acceptance of *us just as we are.*

Let's get concrete about this: How does this really happen in our everyday lives? That's the real question.

Our experiences of everyday living vary quite a lot, but choose one of these, or make up one of your own, and we will trace the movement into mystery that we have been describing here:

- ☐ Someone dies
- ☐ You wake up feeling sick
- ☐ The sunrise is gorgeous
- ☐ You realize that you're gay
- ☐ Your child is in trouble
- ☐ You've just heard a moving poem
- ☐ You feel a little restless today
- ☐ The doctor says you have AIDS or cancer
- ☐ You give an anonymous gift to someone
- ☐ You have an overwhelming sense of well-being
- ☐ You kiss and make up with someone
- ☐ An old friend calls just to visit
- ☐ A song brings back old memories
- ☐ You commit that same old sin again

These are common, everyday, ordinary human experiences. But they hold the potential for divine revelation. How do these experiences lead us to Holy Mystery?

■ THE HOLY PAUSE ■

First, they absolutely cannot do so unless we pause to reflect on them. Pausing is, without question, the first step.

Those who first formed the prayer of the church knew
this in their bones. They established a series of regular
times for prayer in every day. These times, it was hoped,
would lead people to reflect on the mysteries on a regular,
periodic basis, day in and day out.

Unfortunately, two elements in our habit of prayer can
diminish its effect. One element is that it can become so
methodical that people simply "say their prayers," rather
than really praying. Prayer is natural to humans, it is our
natural orientation to pray. We do it all the time, naturally.
It's how we're made: We are oriented to Mystery. The other
way prayer is diminished is when it is reduced to reflection on what are thought to be purely "divine" mysteries.

The divine, holy Mystery is absolutely unfathomable,
incomprehensible, inexhaustible, essentially unsolvable
and wholly other. All that we can know of this Mystery
comes to us through our everyday human experiences.

Everything we say about God is really a statement
about ourselves, someone once observed. But everything
we say about ourselves is also a statement about God.

So pausing to reflect on the mysterious events of ordinary, everyday life, is what will lead us ultimately to the
Holy Mystery we seek. Pausing in our day, several times,
pausing to reflect on the last couple of hours, is the first
step. This Holy Pause doesn't have to take a lot of time:
really two minutes will do it. Pause and ask yourself this

question: What has gone on in this time that holds the potential for Mystery? At first, it might not be easy or obvious, but after you practice it for a while, you'll be amazed at how quickly you'll recognize Mystery.

What has gone on? It might not be major or earth-shaking. Simple things in everyday life can trigger your reflection: a letter in the mail, a song on the radio, a news item from the daily papers, a phone call, a moment in the garden, a glimpse at the photo of a loved one, a memory, an impulse, an urge....

Unless we pause, we will miss the potential for Mystery contained in these moments. We will go rushing on, trying in vain to find meaning, trying to be satisfied, trying to find comfort and rest, when all along, the meaning, the satisfaction of the heart, and the rest we seek, is right there, waiting to be encountered. The Holy Pause is very important.

▪ THE HOLY SHARING ▪

Second, once we have paused to encounter Holy Mystery, we need to share it with someone else and we need to do this often. Once we begin, we will hunger for this daily bread, we will long for this opening, this putting-into-words of the events and experiences of our lives. This is a sort of "everyday mystagogia." Mystagogia is an ancient practice of Christians and others, and it is in essence what we are describing here. In the church, we often reflect on the rites and liturgies we have experienced. But we can also reflect on the whole of life as I'm describing it here.

Sharing like this can take several forms: a phone call or a letter will do it, but the most immediate form, the most energizing form, the most clarifying form, is a simple, personal visit with someone.

Daily Mass surely began this way. It was a time for people to gather, to share their lives. A very appropriate context for this kind of sharing is a daily meal. Families, communities, friends: We can all do this if we want to.

Sharing is important. It takes the otherwise still abstract thoughts and observations of life and puts words on them, makes them concrete, brings them out into reality, gives them air, lets them be challenged, clarified, and owned.

Here's the exciting part: We do this naturally. It's a part of our nature to process our lives this way. But often this processing becomes only chatter, it becomes a news report, a safe, almost antiseptic newsy little summary that doesn't give way to meaning.

Because Holy Mystery both leads us to fear yet lures us toward itself, we tend to avoid the encounter. To encounter Holy Mystery, however, is to encounter our very Selves.

So, like the Holy Pause, this Holy Sharing, can lead us to ultimate meaning and can ultimately lead us to our full Selves. We are quite accustomed to non-talk, to chatter, and some of us will have to re-learn how to share.

So first the Holy Pause and then the Holy Sharing: What's next?

▪ THE HOLY WRITINGS ▪

All of this is rooted beyond the ordinary storytelling of daily life in the Great Stories of our Holy Writings. Here, in the gospels and letters of the Scriptures, we find the Jesus story, which is what nourishes and sustains and gives meaning to our own everyday experience. We need to find a way, on a daily basis, to hear this Word.

But I don't think this means that we have to speed through the text. Rather, taking one story at a time, maybe for a week or more, and letting it sink into our marrow will provide a deeper meaning. Parishes establish a way for members to do this now using what is known as the "question of the week," an ancient practice of the church also known as "breaking open the Word." Let the Gospel penetrate your life.

We need to do more than read it. We also need to study it. Scripture scholarship is readily available today. There is no excuse for any of us not looking beyond the Bible for more. By looking further, we will discover the historical, editorial, literary, faith-filled context in which it was written. These are, after all, the stories of the Community. This also connects with the tradition and doctrine of the church. In a way, this doctrine is a summary of all we humans have already come to understand about the divine indwelling.

This all takes us beyond ourselves, beyond our everydayness, into the great common stories which enlighten our own stories every day.

We will find a rhythm in this: a couple Sacred Pauses in our day, a time of Sacred Sharing with another, a time with the Sacred Stories of Scripture, and finally, gathering now and then with friends and neighbors and family to celebrate all of this with singing and dancing, storytelling, laughing and crying, liturgizing, eating and drinking. We gather ourselves together, the ins and outs of life, the ups and downs. And we bring along the memories, the dreams, and the stories.

We bring it all together in one place with the elements of earth: bread and water and wine, and we summarize life, we celebrate it.

Then this Great and Holy Mystery, which we encounter along our way, yields profound meaning and we realize that without it now, without that encounter each day, we could not go on living. We learn who we really are by reflecting on how we really live and by holding that up against the stories of Scripture. When we are revealed to ourselves in divine revelation that way, those moments of discovery are really moments of grace.

Grace, then, is when God communicates God's own very self to us by revealing us to ourselves—both our guilt and our goodness—in the context of community sharing about everyday events in our lives and the words of Holy Scripture. Grace is an essential part of being human, a "supernatural existential" according to Rahner. It is a fundamental dimension of being human and the first fruit is God's absolutely free self-offer.

3

Grace
EXPOSES OUR
GUILT

We are guilty, yes.
But we are also good.
Grace brings these two elements
into the light.

Do you remember the story about Peter in the courtyard during the trial of Jesus? It's a haunting story if you read it from the point of view of grace.

It is usually thought by preachers, teachers, and others in the know that in the story Peter denied Jesus. In fact, the story itself is often called by that title, "Peter's denial of Jesus." But I have never been convinced that that is what happened there, at least not directly.

The gospel from John's community tells this story of denial most poignantly. In this version of the story, there is a small crowd of folks gathered around a charcoal fire near where the trial of Jesus is taking place. The juxtaposition with the trial is obviously no accident: Peter is on trial, too.

(The charcoal fire is also important, but more about that later.)

Now you must remember that all of the other disciples had run off, frightened. The text tells us that only Peter followed Jesus, and even then at quite a distance. It would be most fair to conclude that Peter was afraid as he stood by that charcoal fire. He was afraid, but at least he was there.

One of the other people there comes up to Peter and tells him the truth: "You are one of them, aren't you?" meaning, "You are the person who lives in company with Jesus."

Remember that this is the gospel in which we have heard Jesus teach us: "You will know the truth and the truth will make you free." But clearly in this case the truth was not making Peter very free, and he denied that he knew Jesus.

But notice, please, he did not deny that Jesus was Jesus, he did not deny that Jesus had been all he'd said he would be. He did not deny Jesus, he denied himself: "I am not," he said, "I am not one of them." He didn't do it just once or twice, he denied himself three times. Obviously, he meant what he said.

This threefold self-denial carries a deep, profound meaning to the hearer of the word. It tells us that Peter was making a profound statement about his own character and self. The threefold statement indicates a deep truth. So the second self-denial was clearly a sign that Peter was locked in himself and locked out of the life of Jesus. But, the third time! Oh, that third time, that is the ultimate time: for now Peter was stepping into a dangerous dark and self-determined hell. The third time, Peter was playing with fire!

(We'll come back to that charcoal fire in a minute.)

■ THE DENIAL OF SELF ■

When I hear this story, I can hear echoing behind it the denial of self that good people throughout the ages have fallen into the habit of practicing. Good people, these, who cannot or will not admit the truth about themselves and who, in the denial of themselves, even though they be "churched" people, deny Jesus.

Deny Jesus?

Yes. That is exactly what we do when we deny who we are. Jesus told us: "I am the truth." That is a powerful self-description. "I am the truth." I am the truth about who you are... what you need... who you love... what you've done... I am the truth about you. So to deny the truth is to deny Jesus. Having faith in Jesus means having faith in the truth means having faith in myself.

I can hear the alcoholic saying "I'm no drunk!" "I'm not an alcoholic." "I am not one of these." (Three times: can you hear the rooster crow?)

I can hear the wealthy people saying "I've earned it!" "But it's all mine." "I am not one of these."

I can hear the self-righteous saying "But she doesn't come to church!" "But he's not in fashion!" "But they're living together in sin!" "I am not one of these."

I can hear the lonely person saying "I'm OK." "Don't bother with me." "I am not one of these."

I can hear the stubborn people saying "I don't have to accept new things." "I don't need to grow." "I am not one of these."

Good people all of these, but people in the habit of denying their very selves. The list goes on: the military bomber the male elite, the nuclear bomb builder, the thief, the liar, the abortionist, the violent, the anti-Semite, the selfish, the grudge-holder, the gossip, the abuser, the apathetic, the faithless, and on and on and on....

Again and again we hear the truth: "Surely you are one of these." And again and again we deny it steadfastly: "I am not," we say, "I am not one of these." But the truth is that we are. We all are. There is no denying it.

Now picture this for a moment: It's a damp, cold night. Why else would you need a charcoal fire? You are standing with a bunch of strangers in a dark alley-like place.

Your best friend is on trial for insisting on doing things that you yourself had tried to talk him or her out of. From nowhere come these strangers accusing you of being part of your friend's crazy carryings-on. Not just once or twice, but three times they accuse you of it. You are frightened, confused, frustrated, cold, and alone. You can't face the fact that this is who you've become. You hadn't noticed that slowly, over the years, this is who you'd really become. You have become one of these. You are in the habit of denying this in yourself because maybe you really don't want this to be true. So when you are confronted like this, you deny that this is who you are.

But in your heart, you know the truth.

A FISH FRY ON THE BEACH

Let's go back to that charcoal fire for a minute. In the story as John tells it, Jesus is convicted, killed, buried, and that's that. The disciples try to get on with their lives. They try, but they are restless. They go from one activity to another, not really able to focus well on anything. They may have gone back to fishing or tax collecting. They may have tried to forget the crazy years of knowing Jesus. They may have tried this—and that—to stay busy: They were trying to forget.

But forgetting someone as dramatic in their lives as Jesus had been would not be easy. He was, after all, the truth of their very lives. He lived within them, as well as alongside them. At the last supper he had offered them bread and wine with the words, "This is my Body. This is my Blood." As Rahner has said, spoken in Aramaic as it was, they knew he was saying, "This is me. I'm offering you myself. I'm donating my own very self to you."

Now the comfort of his physical presence is gone, but not the truths that he'd revealed to them. He haunts them: his words, his actions, his love for them, his friendship, his care, his truth-telling. They just can't forget. They've done the crying. They've talked about him endlessly for days, maybe even for weeks.

Then one night they are sitting down by the sea, the sea that they remember Jesus loved. There are seven of them there: Peter, of course; Thomas, who doubted; Nathanael, the one from Cana; James and John, the sons of Zebedee; and two others but we can't remember who they were. There were seven: it's as though the whole church was there.

It was clearly another one of those nights: They were restless, unable to forget, sulking around, not satisfied, not at ease, not peaceful. One of them would get up. He'd toss a stone into the lake. Then another would wonder aloud where he'd go from here. Then a third would wish again that he hadn't run off, leaving Jesus behind.

Finally Peter, impulsive Peter, had had it. "I can't take it any more!" he said, "I'm getting out of here: Let's go fishing." So off they went. Can't you just see the seven of them:

there in the dark, crowded into a boat designed for three, fishing in the night?

But, that's what they'd been doing with their lives: fishing in the dark. That's what happens when people begin denying themselves: they live in darkness. Then the text of John's Gospel says, as the light began to break someone was standing on the beach. The writer is careful to let us know who it is, but careful to note as well that the fishing party in the story was still in the dark about it: They did not know it was Jesus.

So this guy on the beach says, "Hey! Have you folks caught any fish?" "No," they told him. "This must be a lousy place to fish." These guys had been trying their best to figure all this out. They'd been trying to own up to who they really were. They'd been working hard at working out their lives. And then, when they just couldn't do it any more, they gave up: "I'm just a lousy person, that's all."

Peter's denial of himself there in front of that charcoal fire was a denial that all the followers of Jesus have gone through. All of us have been on trial with Jesus. All of us were being judged: "Are you the person you were created to be?" "Or have you become someone else?" "Isn't this really who you are?" And all of us, all of us, along with Peter, have denied our very selves. It is for all of us a time of great darkness, a dark night of truth.

So here's this guy on the beach telling them now to keep going: "Throw your nets on the other side of the boat!"

Why hadn't they thought of that? I wonder. I mean, these fishers were professionals; they used to do this for a living. Could they possibly have been fishing all night without trying the right side of the boat? But they tried it anyway, one more time, and lo! their nets were filled: one hundred and fifty-three large fish! And that's a lot of fish.

When this happened, John, one of Jesus' closest friends, finally realizes that the guy on the beach is Jesus. The lights come on all around and everyone can see it now. The dawn was upon them.

Haven't we done that? Haven't we recognized Jesus like that?

The text is clear: As the dawn is breaking over our lives, as the light begins to scatter the darkness, as we begin to find our way and make our catch, it will dawn on us: The one calling to us, the one giving the directions, the one standing there unnoticed until now is Jesus. When we finally see that, then we are enlightened. And then, for the first time in our lives, we begin to experience resurrection.

Then the story goes on to say that Peter, impulsive Peter, naked Peter, when he realized that it was Jesus, put on his garments and jumped into the water. We've all done that: We've caught a glimpse of Jesus on the shore, or our parents did, and we put on the garment of baptism and jumped into the waters of new life.

The story goes on to tell us that the very next thing they did together was to share a meal, a breakfast fish fry on the beach.

This is probably the first real meal these disciples have had in days: You know how hard it is to eat when you feel restless. In fact, it's probably their first real meal since that last supper they'd had with Jesus.

And the meal took place over a charcoal fire. It was a meal, no doubt, of thanksgiving: a Eucharist. What were they thankful for? Undoubtedly, they were grateful for each other: for being embraced by this warm, human community of faith. The old solidarity was returned to their company. A sense of hope surrounded them. They were in *his presence* and they knew it.

And it was over that charcoal fire, the same fire over which Peter had run away from himself, and thereby run away from Jesus, over this same fire now, that Peter would come home.

But this isn't the damp, dark night of the trial, alone with strangers, accusing Peter of the truth. No, this is a quiet morning, a gentle lake lapping at the shore, friends, light, a good meal, comfort in being with Jesus. And Jesus confronts Peter with the truth, the same truth he had denied earlier, the truth which is Jesus. But this time it is different. Jesus had already forgiven and accepted Peter in all his stupidity and sinfulness.

This time it is a confrontation in love: "Peter, do you love me?" "Peter, are you one of mine?" "Peter, are you one of these?"

"Yes, my friend," Peter responds, "yes, I am. I am one of these!" And Peter had come home to himself.

—— ■ 4 ■ ——

Grace
IS ENERGIZING

Grace is experienced as a divine power.
It is the power of love.
We are empowered to be
*   our ownmost selves.*

In the story about Peter's denial of himself and, thereby, of Jesus, we learn a great deal about grace and empowerment. The two go hand-in-hand: When Peter finally seized the personal power to be his ownmost self, then he was also simultaneously seized by the grace of Jesus. Indeed, it was the grace of Jesus that enabled him to be his ownmost self in the first place.

All of the gospels are filled with talk about empowerment. From the announcements of the angels, first to Mary and then to the shepherds, to the commissioning of the apostles after the resurrection, the gospels repeatedly refer to the empowerment of God.

Do you remember the time Jesus was in the synagogue? He had gone there after coming out of the desert. The text is clear about this: "Jesus returned in the power of the Spirit," the text says, and then it goes on to tell this story: Jesus went to Nazareth, which was where he'd lived as a child. His adult home was probably in Capernaum so this was like a homecoming for him.

He went to the synagogue, which he was in the habit of doing on the Sabbath day. He stood up to read and he was given a copy of the Scriptures, in particular the book of the prophet Isaiah. The text gives a lot of detail here: He opened the book, he found the place he wanted, he began to read, he read, he closed the book, he gave it back to the attendant, he sat down: a very dramatic storytelling.

But what he read was even more dramatic: "The Spirit of the Lord is upon me," it began, "...he has anointed me, empowered me, to preach, to proclaim release, to give sight, to set free, and to proclaim the year of the Lord." It was no wonder that the eyes of all were fixed upon him after he sat down. This had been a demonstration of tremendous power.

There were many other times in the gospels where this power was demonstrated. For example, one day Jesus had gathered some folks around him; they were attracted to him and to his teachings. On this particular occasion, he taught a large group for a long time on the side of a mountain near his home. We have come to call that occasion "The Sermon on the Mount." After he was finished with his work that day, the text tells us that the people wondered aloud how he could speak with such power, with such authority. In fact, the text says that the people who had heard him that day were absolutely astonished at his power!

That happens sometimes when there is a great speaker: The crowd becomes enthused, energized, filled with power. Only in this case, it was more than that: It was more than merely seeing someone powerful: This crowd was empowered by Jesus.

That is, the power of God, so present in Jesus of Nazareth that day, was not used as a means of over-powering others but rather of *empowering* them. That's why the crowds were so astonished. They simply weren't accustomed to having people in authority do anything but over-power them. Michael Crosby has helped us to see that this way that God has of sharing with us, of empowering us through Christ, this is Grace!

THE POWER TO BE OUR FULL SELVES

And what does this Grace empower us to do? It is the Grace to be our ownmost selves, to be the persons we are meant to be, to live out our created purpose, to come home to ourselves. Just look at the Sermon on the Mount which precedes the astonishment of the crowds:

"Are you poor in Spirit?" Jesus would ask. "Then you have God's favor, God's power, God's grace."

"Are you meek? "Do you hunger for justice? "Are you merciful to others? "Are you a peacemaker?" Jesus would ask. "Then you are filled with God's love, God's power, God's grace."

"Be who you are," Jesus is saying. "Be the person you are created to be." "Be fully yourself." "Anybody who is created by God, which includes all of you, is created to be somebody. Don't become nobody, don't give away this power to be yourself, don't deny my grace to you. Instead, come home to yourselves." It was quite a sermon, wasn't it?

When Jesus described what it is like to be in the kingdom of God, he used a powerful image: "The kingdom," he said, "is within you." "Don't go looking here and there; don't think you can find it outside of yourself. No. The kingdom you seek is within. And, when you find it, it will be like the person who finds a precious gem: You would trade nothing for it!"

How true that is! We search and search for our identity and when we finally find ourselves, created, rooted in Christ, loved eternally, then there is nothing that we would trade!

Later on one time, Jesus had spent some apparently healing time with a young crippled man. The time they spent together was such that Jesus could say to him in the context of their friendship, "Be of good cheer, my friend, your sins are forgiven!" It must have been a great moment for both of them! A time of real intimacy, real sharing, real truth-telling, and, finally, real healing. But some of the religious hierarchy of that day were threatened and offended by this intimacy, this healing, this forgiveness, this reconciliation, and this power. They would have presumed that he was crippled in the first place because of his sins. So they challenged Jesus. "No problem," Jesus told them. "This power I have is to be shared. Here, let me show you." And with that, Jesus empowered this young man to come after him, to follow him, in a word, to take up his pallet and walk.

As he did this, he said he was doing it in order to demonstrate the empowering, unconditional love of God. The text repeats for us, in the very next line, that the crowds were floored! They had seen the power of God, the Grace of God. They were *moved by Jesus.*

And in the very next breath of the text, the very next verse, Jesus calls Matthew from his life of darkness and gives him a new energy, an energy to be his real self, an energy to leave his unreal self behind: the energy of grace. Just imagine the relationship that this line of the text is summarizing: Jesus and Matthew must have spent quite a little time together, enough time, at least, that Matthew, freed by the trust, the acceptance, the honesty, the gaze, of Jesus, could be empowered to make new choices, could be graced to become his real, full, created Self. What a great and powerful thing the love of God, expressed in Christ, can be for us!

The gospel goes on and on in describing the empowerment of God! In the very next chapter, for example, Jesus calls a group of his followers to himself and sends them out to preach and teach and heal. But he doesn't just send them, he empowers them! The text is clear: "He gave them authority...." He empowered them. He gave them Grace.

And at the end of the gospel story, the writer gives the crowning moment in the life of Christ and in the purpose of Christ's life, which was to empower the human family to live up to its real self, its created self. Jesus is pictured with the ones who followed him, and he is preparing them for the work of building the church. In doing this, Jesus sends them to all the nations, invites them to baptize, asks them to teach, and promises to be with them. But, before he does all this, the text tells us, he empowers them! He gives them the grace they will need.

We are very close now to understanding that we are empowered to be our ownmost selves and that, when we accept that empowerment in faith, then we accept Christ as well. Then we become persons-for-others, persons sent to heal, persons empowered for ministry in our everyday lives.

The very stuff of alienation, of sin, of suffering, and of fear in us becomes the stuff that our ministry is made of. "Our weakness becomes our strength."

Then we discover that in the moment of accepting grace and power we become powerless. We discover that we become full only when we are empty. We discover that we will live only when we willingly die. We are the earthen vessel and God's grace is sufficient to sustain and empower us. Nothing else can do that.

And at this moment, this moment of powerlessness and emptiness, something absolutely astonishing happens for us: We experience healing and we begin to become whole again. We experience reconciliation in our lives.

Concretely, this being empowered is a process of taking back responsibility for our own lives. We take back who we really are. We become our ownmost selves again, and we find that our ownmost self is always a self-for-others. This taking-back is done not with hate or anger, but with a profound love, a love that in turn empowers others.

But who do we take it back from? For some it is necessary to regain self from one's spouse. Married people sometimes give each other too much control over their lives. For others it is friends to whom they surrender themselves. For still others it is old memories, old sins, the old days. Some others give themselves to religious groups of various kinds: to cults; to ideologies such as individualism, capitalism, racism, sectarianism, sexism, homophobia, communism, or consumerism. For many it is a favorite compulsion: smoking, drinking, stealing, lying, working, sleeping, praying, eating, or whatever. For most people, how they live is determined by materialism and consumerism. These people allow society to dictate their behaviors and responses. Fashion becomes their god.

Clearly, in order to live in the grace of Jesus, the power of God, and the power of light, we need to take back our life from all these alienating forces around us. We need to become our ownmost selves again.

▪ WE ARE NOT ALONE ▪

Now, I know what's going on inside of you: You're think-ing, "That's easy for you to say! Anybody can tell us this! That's easier said than done!" And you're right, of course. But there is something else here, something that helps to make this circle complete: We are not alone. And Jesus was not alone either. We often misunderstand this in the gospels. We think, "Well, Jesus was God. He was all-pow-erful. He didn't have to deal with life the way I do."

This attitude accounts for a lot of people assuming that Jesus never had to practice what he preached. Jesus is God. No doubt about it. But he is also human, very human, completely human, humanly human.

He ate, drank, slept, sweated, wept, worried, wondered, sang, told stories, worked, got blisters, made mistakes, and generally was a regular type of guy. Jesus was human and he faced all that humans face. He wasn't half human and half divine, Gene LaVerdière has pointed out, not "human on his mother's side and divine on his father's side!" No. He was fully human, fully divine. This is mysterious and hard to understand, but it is also very important.

Let's look at this from the point of view of grace. Jesus was human, born of Mary, and he experienced the grace that all humans can: the grace of first breath, the grace of functioning lungs, the grace of working bowels, in sum, the grace of the energy of life. Grace is experienced in a physical way like that, we know this, and it's why we pray for physical healing when we are sick. It's also why we even have a sacrament of healing in the church.

But there was more. There is more for all of us. Jesus also experienced the immediate power of love, of acceptance, of being cared for by others. What a wonderful power! What a wonderful grace! And growing up in that home, with a mother who was full of grace, full of power, and full of peace, and with a father who was as good as they come, Jesus would experience many other forms of grace: the power of forgiveness, of kindness, of hospitality, of tears, of affection, of sharing, of work, of friendship, of honesty, of prayer, of reading Scripture, of poverty, and of peace.

All of this grace, all working together, channeled through those others with whom he shared life. This grace filled Jesus, filled him full of grace and power.

So it came as no surprise, I would imagine, to those who knew him well, that when he began to speak, his words were also full of power, and that when he began to heal, his acts were full of power as well. I would think that anyone who knew him would not have been surprised at all that he would have been a peacemaker, a lover, a healer, a teacher, and, above all, a friend to those he lived among.

This is the point: Grace, which is God donating and communicating God's own self to us, comes through the powerful acts of those around us, the acts of love, selflessness, forgiveness, and affection. This grace, of which Jesus was full, this grace is the life of God. The life of God is itself powerful, creative, and energizing, and Jesus was full of that power!

Grace is an energy. It is not a mere theology. It far more than a mere thought of God, or even word of God. A metaphor for this is the energy of electricity. It courses through us, electrifying our lives! It is indeed a divine energy. It is the energy of divine love, rolling into our lives like waves, never-ending tides, toward the shores of human need.

God gave God's self to the world in this wonderful, yet almost frightening way. "God so loved the world," the text says, "that God sent that one which was most a part of God's own self: Jesus."

Do you realize what this means? This means that God's own life, God's energy, God's grace is within us. And it means that we are empowered, (empowered!) to energize others by loving them, forgiving them, accepting them, and creating them. This is no small thing. The powerful ones we know are usually said to be the ones with money, with importance, or with guns.

But we are talking here about a power far greater than that! This is a power that can do marvelous things: It can heal, bind together, give comfort, offer affection, rest peacefully, create new persons, forgive, and if we would ever really accept this power, the way that Jesus and Mary did—accept it completely and embrace it with our whole selves—then we could also forge a new way for the human family to live together: then it would feed the hungry, give drink to the thirsty, visit the imprisoned, clothe the naked, and heal the sick. No other power will do it. This is all we've got.

5

Grace
EXPOSES OUR
GOODNESS

We humans have bodies.
But we are often ashamed
of our own skin.
Grace opens a new horizon as it
exposes our bodily goodness.

Something that has always been very striking to me is that, even though it is true that in the gospel story Jesus died naked, I rarely see a crucified image of him without clothing. Jim Lopresti has helped us understand that this is a curious reinterpretation of the gospel on the part of the ones in charge of making our images; probably zealous people who must think that it would be "impure" to picture Jesus naked.

Like most of us, these good people are likely afraid of their own nakedness, both emotional and physical, and so believe that they must deny Jesus his. We have probably done this in order to prevent "perverts" from distorting the gospel and desecrating Jesus but in the very act of prevention, we have ourselves created a worse distortion than we have prevented.

The text easily supports that it is true that Jesus died naked. And more, the tradition of crucifixion from the first century also suggests that it is true. The text makes a point of telling us explicitly that they stripped Jesus and that they gave his clothing away. And that he died alone and naked is clearly part of the point of the story in the Gospel of Mark.

In this Markan version the arrest of Jesus has an interesting twist that can help us appreciate the importance of how Jesus died.

It seems that the soldiers came armed with weapons to seize Jesus. By itself, this does seem a bit odd, as Jesus himself is said to have remarked, since he was present in the temple almost every day, teaching and healing. They could have nabbed him on any day.

But anyway, that is how they came, with swords and clubs, a fierce band of soldiers with Judas in the lead. Judas came forward, as he'd planned to do, and got the ball rolling by kissing Jesus. Immediately they laid hands on him and seized him! For the first time, violent hands were laid on the peacemaker! And how odd that it should have started with a kiss! The text tells us that all who were with him forsook him and fled.

Were these the same ones who had just broken bread with him? Were these the same ones who had been attracted enough to Jesus to have left their personal lives behind them in order to join with him? Were these the same ones who had been his friends? I think they were. But, nonetheless, off they ran....

But here comes the twist: one man seemed to linger, he was a young man, clothed only in some kind of linen cloth, the kind in which people are baptized...and buried. Did the writer intend for him to represent all the rest of us? The text tells us that the soldiers seized him but that he wriggled out of his linen cloth, wriggled out of his baptism, wriggled out of his call-to-death, and fled. But the text is explicit in making the point that he ran off naked. Why is this so important?

To the audience of the first century it carried a deep meaning.

Clothing gives a person identity. This is true today but it was especially true in the first century when this text was written. By using that symbol, nakedness, the writer of that story starts redefining what it means for Jesus to Reign as Ruler of All. The Christian Scripture is filled with stories of nakedness and clothing.

Jesus was wrapped in swaddling clothing on the night of his birth. This was no accident: The author of that text is telling us that Jesus was earthy, human, poor, of the "humus."

John the Baptizer always wore the garment of Elijah because it best represented the mission of his life as the last and connecting prophet. At the Transfiguration, the story tells us that Jesus was clothed in a garment that showed his glory. The young man sitting in the tomb after the resurrection wore this same white garment to properly announce Jesus' victory over death. Paul speaks of "putting on Christ like a garment."

Clothing made the person. It announced to all who the person was, what role the person would play, and what attitude the person took. Clothing made you somebody because it identified you as more than nobody. So when this young man ran away naked at the time of the arrest of Jesus, he ran away as a nobody. Baptism had made him somebody but leaving Jesus had made him a nobody.

But before we explore these important connections let's examine two more stories about clothing in the gospels.

■ THE PRODIGAL SON ■

The first is the story of the Prodigal Son. When this runaway son came home to ask his father's forgiveness, he had a plan made and a speech written. The text is in Luke's Gospel. In his little rehearsed speech, the son planned to offer to return as a servant, as a slave, as a hired hand. In the days when Jesus told this story, it would have been very clear to his audience that this would mean that he would not wear the clothing of a son because, for the most part, servants, especially field slaves, worked naked, worked as nobodies. The audience would have found this to be really something! The son of a landowner, the son of a nobleman, working as a servant! dressing as a slave! That would really have been remarkable!

So here comes the son down the road with the father running out to meet him. The kid begins his speech: "Dad, I know that what I've done can never be undone and I know that I have broken your heart and no longer deserve to be called your son...." But the father interrupts him. And what does the father say? "Quick! Get a garment for my son! A ring for his finger! Sandals for his feet! Dress him! Why? Because my son has returned!" To the audience of the first century, that said it all.

Is this really a story about two young people, the "good son" and the "prodigal son"? Or is it really a story about one young man with two competing inner voices, one voice urging him to be at home with himself and God and the other urging him away from himself and God? The text tells us that while he was away from "home" the young man "came to his senses" which means, I think, that he realized, finally, that he was not living as he was created to live, that he was not being his full self. His decision to return "home" was at once a decision to return to himself. But even after he got there, that other nagging voice, the one of the "good son," kept him from forgiving himself. The "good son" in us, often holds more against us than the "father" does.

■ THE MAN WITH DEMONS ■

In another place in this same gospel, there is another story about clothing that will help us to understand even more deeply how important this symbol is for us. In this story, a "man with demons" meets Jesus one day just as Jesus is landing in a boat. This guy, the text tells us, had spent years living among the tombs, among the dead, and he had worn no clothing. He lived naked. He was nobody.

We are given to believe that this guy is insane, screaming awful things and frightening the people. The text does not say this but I think it would be fair to conclude that all of us are insane sometimes. All of us are screaming inside and from time to time we scream outside, too.

Jesus knew how this felt; he had felt that way himself. His presence to this man was a healing one, a presence that would "drive those demons out" of the man. As the story goes, the local workers, frightened by all of this, go tell the townspeople who, as might be expected, rush out to see what had happened. I can just see them coming down the road toward the lakefront where all this had taken place. They want to know who this Jesus is and what happened to those demons. When they get there, the text tells us, they found Jesus all right but they also found this fellow that Jesus had healed, and the text is explicit in saying that they found him clothed and sitting at the feet of Jesus. He had met the power of Jesus; he was no longer nobody; he was no longer naked; now he was clothed because now he was somebody!

All of this helps us to understand that when Jesus was stripped and when he died naked the people were saying that he was nobody special to them. And all of this helps us to understand one kind of nakedness in the Scriptures: "the nakedness of nobodiness."

This is the kind of nakedness that people experience often in their lives. It is a nakedness of distortion, sin, rupture, violence, and meanness. People who are raped are made naked in this way: the nakedness of nobodiness. Rape, inside or outside of marriage, renders people as nobodies. People who are victims of gossip are made naked in this way. Even when the facts being reported in the gossip are true, still, a person is being emotionally stripped without his or her consent; they are being made naked as though they were nobody. People who use others for casual sex, sex without commitment, are stripping others in this way, even when the other gives consent to the sex. They are not saying to that person: "You are really somebody to me!" They are saying, instead, "You are nobody, really; I just want to have sex." The nakedness of nobodiness is everywhere in our society today.

But, thank goodness, it is not the end of the story.

We're going to come back to this in a moment, but first, we need to talk about another kind of nakedness, "the nakedness of somebodiness."

It is impossible to read the story of creation in Genesis and not realize that God created the human body naked, unclothed, in all its glory! The creation of the human body, including the sexual parts, is not the result of "the fall" in the story. But rather, as Fran Ferder has pointed out, it is the culminating high point of all of creation!

Whether you read the story as literally true or as symbolically relevant, you come to the same conclusions: The human body was God's idea. Now get this: Rather than nakedness being the result of the so-called fall, clothing is! It is easy to see that going naked is God's idea while wearing clothing is, in a pretty significant way, a symbol of our sinfulness.

And that's why, when we reach the pinnacle of love with someone, we take off all our clothing and lie naked together. We touch one another, marvel in one another's beauty, affirm one another, love one another deeply. It is at these moments that we experience the "nakedness of somebodiness."

Now we are naked, not because we are nobody to this person, but because we have really become somebody special, important, unique, individuated, significant, and holy. This physical nakedness is powerful, creative, and life-giving because it is not selfish. It is a physical nakedness which has been preceded by emotional nakedness. The sharing of dreams, ideals, desires, fantasies, feelings, and commitments has rendered each person emotionally naked. The physical nakedness which follows upon that is only natural because it is a symbol or expression of the intimacy of emotional nakedness. This is a nakedness that we long for, dream about having, and work toward.

There is a book in the Hebrew Scriptures that tells this story better than any other. It is the Song of Songs. This is the story of a love affair. It is a collection of lyric poetry which is graceful, sensuous, and erotic and it is included here in the Bible because this level of nakedness returns us to an understanding of our primary relationship with God, and therefore with one another, as a relationship in which the "nakedness of somebodiness" is the highest form of expression.

It is an interesting footnote on this commentary that in some Christian churches, readings from the Song of Songs are omitted from the regular cycle of liturgical texts, presumably because they are so erotic! In the Roman lectionary, these texts are included only for the feast of St. Mary Magdalene who was thought to be a prostitute! (A careful reading of Scripture, by the way, does not support that thought.) But what are we saying as a church by suggesting even indirectly, that being erotic is material only for reformed prostitutes? The exclusion of these texts and the general exclusion of preaching on love and love-making have to be a starting point for us now as we continue to consider grace and nakedness.

▓ FORGIVENESS MADE REAL ▓

You see, Jesus, when he was hanging there naked on the cross, took the nakedness of nobodiness with which they intended to kill him, and transformed it into the nakedness of somebodiness. In doing this, Jesus undid what had happened in the story of the garden in the Book of Genesis. On the cross, in the midst of violence, rejection, hatred, abuse, ridicule, and apparent failure (all the stuff of which nobodies are made) Jesus responded with forgiveness.

He took the opposite action. We should not be surprised to hear this. After all, this is the same Jesus who, time after time, confused the crowds (and us) by teaching that we must die in order to live, must give in order to receive, must be weak in order to be strong. Now he is teaching us that we must forgive, in order to end violence, the violence that creates the nakedness of nobodiness.

Now, when you hear the word "forgiveness" if you are a Catholic, and probably even if you aren't, you likely think of confession where people used to go to "get forgiveness" (which was a pastoral abuse, not a theological position of the church). Try to forget that connection. Forgiveness, Jim Lopresti has said, happens before the sin, not after it. It is a "givenness before." It is a permanent attitude. It is an unconditional positioning of one person toward another. Confession is the celebration of that fact that we are already forgiven by God!

Rahner has pointed out that God offers us unconditional acceptance, an offer from God that seems too good to be true. This is the most fundamental offer that God makes to us.

Jesus forgave his killers, which is to say that he gave up any claims that he had on them for the pain, embarrassment, false charges, and even death that they caused him. He gave up his claims on them, which means that he held nothing against them, which is the key part of forgiveness. Jesus' forgiveness of them was a powerful, creative act.

Pilate once told Jesus, "Don't you know that I have the power to free you or the power to have you killed." Jesus responded: "You have no power over me."

When Jesus said that, this is what he was talking about. By forgiving them, Jesus gave them no power. Even as they were acting, even as they were exercising their "power," Jesus was taking it all away from them and rendering them powerless. What could they do to him?

In doing this, Jesus was saying that God had no claims on us, either. For God, the first exercise of power was in creation: the creation of the human person, the energizing of human persons with life, and the energizing of the world with Spirit. And the second exercise of power for God was in donating this creation to us, especially in the person of Jesus, his ownmost self, now present with us. It's amazing when you think of it that God would not have hung on to all that had been created. But God made absolutely no claims on creation, giving it all to us. God gave up all claims even on the human family, rightful though those claims would have been.

That is, God gave up God's own rightful claims on creation, gave humans their freedom to live, to love, and to listen to God as they want.

So Jesus, in giving up his rightful claims on the cross, transformed nakedness. Now, rather than being a naked nobody, Jesus was a naked somebody because he was loving us with the kind of love that lovers know. He was expressing total vulnerability, total unconditionality, total presence. There has been no more dramatic expression of love in the history of the world! And Jesus' own great act of forgiveness has freed us and has procreated in us the power for forgiveness, which is the power to transform the world.

For us this is grace: We spoke already about the power to be our ownmost selves. Now we are speaking about the power that comes from Jesus' word of forgiveness: When you are stripped by gossip: forgive. When you are violated by rape: forgive. When you are victimized by violence: forgive. When you are stunned by murder: forgive. When you are an object of lust: forgive.

When you are hurt, rejected, ridiculed, spat upon, or even killed: forgive. Do not give your enemies power over you by holding claims against them. Forgive the oppressors, forgive the racists, forgive the sexists, forgive the communists, forgive them all!

This is the mystery of the cross for us: Jesus says on that cross: "Do you think this will keep me from loving you? Do you? Do you think this'll stop me?"

It's really very impractical, forgiveness is. If you forgive, you'll be done in for sure. But that's the point: If getting done in doesn't bother you, then what have you got to lose? What's left to hurt you? You will then have absolute freedom.

Now, a footnote: This does not mean that we are ever excused from working for peace and justice in the world. By describing one who forgives, we are not describing one who is passive in the face of oppression, violence, and evil. There is a great misunderstanding about the death of Jesus that floats about certain religious circles from time to time. Some people believe that Jesus was simply passive in allowing himself to be killed. This notion comes from a mistaken view of the humanity of Jesus. Jesus was fully human; he did not, from time to time wander between humanity and divinity. He was full of the energy of grace, which enabled and empowered him to live his full life, which is the life of God, but he did not exercise this power unilaterally. That was his point.

Don't you remember the taunting of the soldiers, "If you are really God, come down from that cross"? By believing that Jesus could have stopped the killers if he'd only wanted to, we participate in that taunting! Jesus could not have stopped them: He was fully human.

What Jesus did in that moment was far from passive! Yet, there are those who believe that somehow being passive in the face of suffering would be acceptable in our day. These believe that by suffering silently like that a person can identify most closely with the suffering of Jesus. "You should accept suffering," these would say, "because that suffering identifies you with Jesus."

But no, we would say, based on this understanding of Jesus and Grace, that we do not have to suffer any longer because of the suffering of Christ!

Just consider: The overall tone of the gospels, and of the approach of Jesus, was to do everything that is humanly possible, empowered with the love of God, to remedy evil.

We are not called to be passive in the face of injustice. Quite the contrary, we are obliged to carry one another's burdens, bear one another's sorrows, and provide for one another's needs.

And for those whose claims have been systematically taken away by others, we must work to restore them at once! There is no mistaking it.

Let's return now to our central line of thinking in this chapter: All of us are victims of nobodiness. All of us are rendered naked by insensitive or evil persons over whose actions we do not always have control. All of us have run off to be wanton, like the prodigal child in the story. All of us are slaves sometimes, choosing to be nobody or to make somebody else into a nobody for our supposed benefit.

How can we transform that? The lesson is the one we've just learned from Jesus' own transformation. Because, for all of us, all of us, the power of forgiveness can restore us, can remake us, can reconcile us, and we can become somebody again!

6

Grace
IS ORDINARY

Grace is a daily experience.
But we must be aware and conscious.

I think it was Will Rogers who once said that life is just one damn thing after another. We want to talk about that next. People live their lives every day. On the face of it, that may seem like kind of an obvious thing to say. But think about it for a minute: Our lives are filled with commonness, with ordinariness, with repetition, with mundane earthiness, with everydayness. We live every day: We get up, we get through the bathroom routine, we get a bite to eat, we get on with the tasks of the day, we get back to work, we get finished, we get to supper, we get some time in the evening, we get to bed.

In the midst of all this, How are we supposed to see the glory of God every day? How are we supposed to recognize the grace and power of God every day? How on earth are we supposed to recognize the Reign of God as it breaks into our lives every day?

Some folks would say that daily Mass, regular prayer times, spiritual direction, joining a prayer group, volunteering in the parish, or having sacred things around the house are the ways to recognize The Reign of God in their lives. But it is possible that if we are too busy with all of those other things we may miss it completely. If we stay busy with activity, with parish duties, with busyness, we may miss seeing God.

In order to recognize the grace we speak of here, we must step back from programs, structures, organizations, and hierarchies, in a word, from churchiness. We need to step back in order to gain perspective on things spiritual. We need to step back in order not to take too much for granted in this constantly surprising part of our lives. We need to step back in order to forget ourselves. The kind of experience of grace that we will talk about here is one, after all, that even the unchurched have on a very regular basis and that sometimes the most churched miss completely.

So we're not talking here only about people who attend Sunday liturgy, only about people who say their prayers, only about church "insiders," or only about "faithful" Christians. We're talking as well about all those others who also experience God in their lives, even when they don't call it that or even when they don't admit that. We're also talking about those parts of life that sometimes seem remote from God, those parts that don't seem to have anything to do with the traditional ways that we have come to understand the work of God in our lives.

▪ SPEAKING OF GOD ▪

Let's begin by thinking together about God. Where is God? We have always been taught that God is "out there" wherever that is, or we've been taught that God's in heaven. When we fold our hands, we were told as children, we point them heavenward toward God. When we build church steeples, we raise them toward God. We carry around inside of us a sense that God is distant from us. We may even feel that God is mainly absent. We have to summon "him" in order to pray. We may have the sense that when it comes to everyday life God is an "outsider."

But nothing could be further from the truth. And this belief, that our God is an outsider god, which the church itself has had a large hand in forming as a popular belief, this belief is one major source of pain, suffering, sickness, alienation, and division. We must do all we can to move forward, to grow in our understanding, but more importantly, to grow in our experience, of the God who is an insider in our lives.

The key to a deeper understanding of grace in our daily lives is to consider how we speak about what happens to us. We go along in our lives, living every day in a willy-nilly sort of way. We don't think much about our common tasks, ideas, conversations, or events. They all just happen, day in and day out, one thing after another.

When we discuss the mundane parts of daily life, we use a simple, straightforward language. "We drove here." or "We ate that." or "We talked with so-and-so. or "We did this today." We talk about the everyday, common events and things of our lives with an everyday, common language. Nothing fancy, just plain old words.

But, for certain parts of our lives, those plain old words just aren't enough. They feel insufficient to describe the deeper realities and profound experiences we have. Then you hear us say, "I just can't tell you how much this means." or "Words just can't describe how I feel." or "There's no way I could tell you how important this is."

And we mean precisely what we are saying: We've run out of language, run out of the words we need to describe certain experiences in our lives. It's as though we've come to the end of words. Plain words can no longer explain the experience or express the feelings. We are simply left speechless by whatever happened.

What experiences might cause this? Maybe a sunrise, a warm expression of affection from someone or an overwhelming, spontaneous sense of well-being. Maybe a death, or a birth, news of an illness, or a phone call from an old friend. Maybe the love we have for our spouse or partner or child, the anxiety we feel about this or that in our lives, or even the hatred, anger, or resentment we feel in the face of this or that. Many experiences may cause this speechlessness.

These experiences are no longer ordinary, common, everyday experiences for us. Because we notice them in a special, observant way, they begin to take on new meaning. They become full of meaning for us. We begin to identify these experiences as important, as unique to us: We begin to see that they are what makes us truly human. They are no longer simply raw human experiences, undefined and unrefined, but now they are dignified, lived, and wholly us. Even if the feelings are negative or selfish, they still fill us with meaning.

These moments are too beautiful, terrible, mysterious, lovely, peaceful, wonderful, frightening, tremendous, and alluring to ever adequately be described in mere words.

They push us to our outer limits, to the edge of the ordinary, to our boundaries, to our deepest depths. We aren't sure how to respond, how to talk or act. We can't explain how we feel because the ordinary language is not sufficient. But who has a language that is sufficient?

We are tempted to try to explain these things fully, but we cannot. We would not ask for a scientific explanation of love because, while it might be accurate, scientifically speaking, it would not be loving. No. To describe love, we would ask a poet, an artist, a painter, a sculptor, or a music writer. But the language of the poet is not ordinary, common language to us. It is a language that seems to come from the other side.

The other side?

Yes, the other side. We are beginning to speak now about God, that one who is on the Other Side. But we must be careful to note that, while God is on the Other Side, God is not, thereby, on the outside.

When we finally face the fact that we've gone beyond the ordinary, we stand at the edge of what we know and can control, and we peer over that edge into the unknown; and we ask, sometimes we shout, the Ultimate Questions: What is over there? Do we dare to go there? Will we find there some way to express the truth hidden in the depths of our souls? Will this give meaning to our lives? Can we endure? What does all this mean? Is anyone there?

So we stand at the edge, peering over into the darkness, feeling at once lured beyond yet frightened to go there. These are very key moments in our lives, and they happen with frequency, although not always with the same force. These can be the moments of grace in our lives.

It is as though we face our true selves in these moments, our full and true selves, and we gather all of that self together, gather in the rough and the smooth, and have the opportunity, an opportunity offered to everyone, to be transformed, to be moved, to be transfixed, to be made whole: and therefore to be made holy.

Let me remind you: These are not usually moments that can be scheduled in the parish bulletin. They are moments, rather, that catch us, grip us, hold us, almost beg us to take notice and thereby be moved beyond.

The trick, we began here by saying, is to listen for them. By using the word "listen" here we mean to say that we need to pause, often, in the daily on-goings of life, pause to reflect on what is going on: the person who called by phone, the letter we received today, the beauty that is rushing past our car windows, the people we are meeting on the streets, the kiss we received and gave this morning, the illness we are experiencing today, that article in the news about that child, this or that, all stuff from our everyday lives: we need to pause to notice it, reflect on it, let it touch us, let it move us.

This really isn't very complicated: For example, you go to lunch with a friend, but instead of talking only about "the weather," instead of chattering on about nothing important, you talk instead about what's really going on. You explore your life. You ask tough questions. You ask the ultimate questions.

What you have when you do this, is a moment of grace. What began as lunch, can end as eucharist (with a lower case "e"), or reconciliation or healing. Only when we are touched and moved by the everyday events and people of our lives, can we be touched and moved by God, whoever he or she may be. That is why the busyness of our lives can be an obstacle, a defense mechanism against the honesty, intimacy, and holiness of crossing over and moving beyond the ordinary.

You see, as we stand on that awe-full edge, peering over to the Other Side, we must make a terrible choice. No one and nothing can ever force us to move beyond that edge. We must choose to do it. The choice, the terrible choice, then, is to go beyond or to turn back.

Many of us will turn back. We turn to cope the best we can, and we invent ways to make that coping possible for us. We may use alcohol to cope, or drugs, meaningless sex, work, busyness, intellectualism, consumerism, partying, machismo, or eating. We turn back to lose ourselves in compulsion rather than move forward to find freedom on the Other Side. The turning back becomes a habit, some would say a religion. By turning back, we pass through the same experiences of self-discovery, sexual discovery, death or birth, beauty, horror, pain, or wonder but instead of being led to Meaning by them, we turn around in fear and do not reflect on them, do not allow them to form us, do not admit our feelings, do not share them with others, do not come out into the open, but rather we hide.

Sometimes we are afraid: Others will think that we "just couldn't handle it." We don't want to appear to be a fool, or worse, a weakling. We don't want to appear dependent on anyone, or needy or confused or, and here's the key: vulnerable. So instead, we bury it all inside ourselves and try to go on as though nothing had happened. What fools we can be! We can never just go on. We are constantly changed. We are always being formed.

So as we stand at the edge, the other choice, the opportunity we have, is to give meaning to the stuff of life by leaping into what is apparently darkness but, we discover, is really Light. We do that by embracing these experiences, admitting the feelings, sharing ourselves with others, dealing with the joy and pain, and finding, on the Other Side, the language to adequately describe all of that, and, therefore, to own it and to let it become a part of ourselves.

In short, we cross over by telling our story and by letting our stories be made meaningful as they're shared among others. You see, we can't share alone. We know that we can't, we know that we don't have the words. But we can find the words, the language we need, on the Other Side. And there have been people telling their stories like this for centuries. We are certainly never alone as we struggle to find words to describe our experiences. We are not alone. We have, for starters, the authors of the Scripture. We have the early mothers and fathers. We also have our neighbors, friends, family, and even strangers who appear in our midst. We have to become vulnerable, we have to admit our story is true.

THE LANGUAGE OF LITURGY

This language of the Other Side is not ordinary. It is transcendent: the language of liturgy, of two people sharing, of poetry, of all kinds of music, painting, silence, touch, imagination, crying and tears, truth-telling, and a whole theater of language that expresses meaning. All taken together, this is called religious language.

There is a strange and powerful mystery in this: In order to cross over, thereby encountering the Other, whom we name God, we must give up ourselves.

There is a kind of dying we must do as we stand at that edge, peering over. We give up our ordinary self in order to receive in return a transformed Self. This dying is the key. Unless we are willing to die to ourselves, we should not expect to find this new life.

It is a strange mystery and mystery is incomprehensible: That is its nature. This cannot be explained: It can be pointed to, we can build ritual around it, we can probe it theologically, but, ultimately, it remains mystery.

But what does this mean? "to die...." It means, really, that we become vulnerable, we become open, we stop the hiding and lying, we face the truth once and for all, we let go the controls. Dying like this is very scary business. We are both drawn to it, yet frightened of it. In all of this, we are listening for the voice of God, speaking not from a roaring fire, not from an earthquake, but from a tiny breeze of wind.

God speaks to us, not many words, as Rahner has said, but one basic word, a word divinely spoken. That word is nothing less than the life of the one who prays in this way, continually drawn into God.

Listening to God in this way means listening to our lives as lives being drawn into the divine mystery. We become now, not a word, but rather a Word spoken by God. Our Self is transformed now so that even the ordinary to which we return and in which we live will never be the same again!

This whole, simple process of naming our experiences in life, of coming to the edge, of facing the ultimate questions, of choosing to turn back or go beyond is something we often face alone. But for those who choose to move beyond, for those who choose to die to self, this journey to the heart of the Lord will not ever be traveled alone. And this is our point here: We are graced, everyone is graced, empowered, in other words, to move beyond and be transformed. And the grace is communicated to us in the community which is the Body of Christ.

This community, the church, excels at providing the ritual and language of the Paschal Mystery. It is a community, the family of God. In this setting, we explore both our guilt and our goodness, under the inspiration of the Holy Spirit. In the church we celebrate sacraments, which are visible, audible, tangible points of contact for us with the mystery of God.

This is such a powerful reality that we can scarcely scratch its surface in attempting to describe it here. But this much is very clear: We must bring ourselves to each other, wounded or rejoicing, vulnerable in any case, bring ourselves to each other, giving ourselves away in intimacy, trust, and faith. What we receive back will be our full transformed whole and Holy Self.

7

Grace
AND SIN

*Each of us must confront
his or her guilt.
But our nature is transformed
by the grace of Jesus Christ.
We know the goodness of God.*

In order to understand grace we've got to talk about sin. The norm we will use here will not be the law. As we will see, we can sometimes follow the law to its letter, and still commit serious sin. Following the law, as Jesus pointed out many times, is no sure route to the Kingdom of God. Seeking the truth means examining the heart, and examining the heart will sometimes support the law but will sometimes challenge the law.

This will be an examination of conscience, and our starting point will be our graced existence as children of God and our ability to discern, both as a church community and within our hearts, where we are alone with God whose voice echoes in our depths. We have seen repeatedly what that means: To be graced is to be all that we are created to be. The created self is not self-made, self-determined, or self-centered. The created self is a self-for-others, self-open-unto-mystery.

The question must always be: "Is this act, judgment, attitude, motive, is it really me?" We don't mean here a me centered on me, but a created me, centered, therefore, in mystery and discovered in relationship to God and others. Does it lead me to Christ? Does it deepen my communion with others? Does it reflect my graced self?

To be human is to be graced, we have said. This means that we all experience the communication of God's own self to us. That is, our self-understanding is in God. We can, in short, know and possess ourselves. We also can communicate ourselves to others. In fact, it is in our very nature to do so. Likewise, we can receive the self-communication of Holy Mystery.

In this experience of grace and life, there is light— but there is also darkness: systems that oppress people, unjust structures, temptations to live for ourselves, subtle manipulation in intimacy, insensitivity, destructive competition, escapism, compulsion, dishonesty.

The "letter of the law" approach to sin and grace has

gotten us into some trouble. We've forgotten to explore grace as it is being poured into our lives, which is much more difficult than keeping the letter of the law. It would not be possible for you to show me in Scripture where it was ever suggested, even remotely, that keeping the letter of the law would somehow be enough for the followers of Jesus. The very opposite is true: The Gospels present the law as a guide but if the law is unloving, then Jesus himself evaluated that negatively.

It was legal, for example, to stone a woman caught in adultery. Legal to make certain offerings in the Temple area. Legal to shun certain people. But Jesus' claim on the people of that age and on us is to go further. Let's look at some examples.

KEEP HOLY THE LORD'S DAY

Let's start by talking about Sunday. Remember Sunday? The letter of the law tells us that we should get to church on Sunday. But getting to church in no way fulfills our "obligation." There have been two extremes with this: those who fulfill the minimal obligation (go to church but nothing else) and those who insist that nothing else should be done that day but formal prayer. Neither is right.

We live our lives in time, running always against the clock. Our lives are full of cares for food, shelter, pleasures. We spend our time, so much of it, planning to buy and buying that sometimes it seems we run into a wall, unable to relax, unable to let go, controlled by the demands of time and attention to the details of daily life.

Sunday puts an end to all of that. It floats somewhere outside of time: We needn't keep schedules on Sunday. And it floats somewhere outside of space: Our cares can be suspended for one day, can't they? We need a day to float and Sunday is that day. Keeping holy the Sabbath means letting go of cares. It means having time to do things that we normally would not: visiting family, calling on the neighbors, taking a nap, sitting around—in a word, killing time. Not a bad idea, that, for people as concerned with time as we are. Sunday is a Holy Pause, and not to have paused is not to have kept holy the Sabbath, no matter how many times you've been to church. And it is all of this pausing that gives us time for reflection on how we live the rest of our lives.

■ SAY YOUR PRAYERS ■

Let's talk now about other times of prayer. When we were children, we were probably taught that it was a sin to miss our daily prayers. I think that's true. We've said earlier here that taking several Holy Pauses each day would allow us to find ourselves in the revealing presence of Holy Mystery.

I once knew a saintly old priest who prayed the Divine Office by working very hard at it. Sometime about 11:00 PM, after a long day of ministry, he'd sit down to begin "saying" the Office and he'd start with morning prayer for the day just ending! Then he'd move on to the rest, finishing finally about midnight just making the deadline! He prayed maybe a dozen psalms, countless Scripture readings, refrains, and antiphons: But he got it all done on time, and that's what mattered.

But then, and here's the amazing part, if he happened to get done early, he'd get himself some ice cream, watch the late show, and wait for midnight. Then he'd start on the next day's prayers, beginning with morning prayer for the day that started after midnight! Then he'd move on and sometimes get all the way through Compline of that day, all in an effort to be sure he got it done, to be sure he worked at it. By doing this, he met every demand of the law about prayer. He did everything according to the minimal obligation based on church teaching. But was it really prayer?

I knew this priest well, by the way, and knew that he also punctuated his day with pauses for prayer, not the official prayer, but something very meaningful. This form of prayer, in which he'd simply pause to feel God's presence before his next appointment, or to wonder at beauty, or to recall someone in need, this was his "real" prayer, and he never knew it.

■ DO NOT BE GREEDY ■

Moving on, this is a tough one: Whatever serves as our ultimate goal becomes our god. For many of us, that ultimate goal, often sleeping beneath the surface, unwilling to rear its ugly head, difficult for us to admit, embarrassing when it appears, is materialism. There is little in human experience more captivating. We have, buried within our human spirit, a constant desire for "more." By itself, there is nothing wrong with that. In the story of the garden in Genesis, the people had all they could have wanted: food, a place to live, companionship, life with God. What else is there really? But they wanted more.

And the drive for more, drove them eventually away from themselves, from each other, and, therefore, away from God's presence.

The very trait of human experience described in that story is the one that keeps most of us from ever seriously following Jesus. We hate to admit this, but we know it's true. This human desire for more, mistaken as a desire for more stuff, is really a desire for more authenticity, more companionship, more intimacy, more love and laughter, more kindness, and more peace.

And the thing about this is that the authentic "more" which we really seek is very close to us. It is the Kingdom which is actually within us.

▪ BE CHASTE ▪

We have been taught that it is always wrong to be vulnerable. Yet personal vulnerability is the key to sexual loving and intimate human fulfillment. When we speak of intimate love, we mean the larger reality which includes intimacy, the sharing of time and space, common possessions, the gaze of love, long talks and walks, mutual other-centeredness. But to speak of love in this way is to suggest that each of the persons is vulnerable to the other. Scripture often refers to intimate loving as "being known" by one another. That being known is very close to the reality we are describing here. To be known is to be exposed, to be open, to take risks, to be honest, completely honest, in a word, to be known is to be exposed.

This vulnerability, this is our most true Self, our created and creating Self. In the creation story of Genesis, it was the crowning high point of all that God had done, and we can easily see why.

Fornication with strangers leaves us invulnerable: We may not even know each other's names. Rape makes only one person vulnerable, and in a completely inappropriate way. Adultery trespasses a bond, creating a unilateral vulnerability rather than a mutual one. Manipulative intercourse or intercourse used to punish even in marriage, removes the vulnerability and places one in power over the other. Prostitution sets up a transaction in which no one is vulnerable to anyone although both are vulnerable to pain. Seduction allows a person to guard his or her vulnerability while another is exposed. Promiscuity seals a person in invulnerability allowing no opportunity for any kind of relationship whatsoever. Pornography institutionalizes invulnerability, making it hard, cast in concrete, impenetrable.

Sin is what keeps us from living out our created purpose. But, as we have also seen here, we are empowered to move beyond sin, and moving beyond sin, which is to live in Christ, will make us whole.

8

Grace
AND PRAYER

God speaks to us in prayer,
not many words
  (such as we speak toward God)
but one divine word:
  the very life of the one who prays.

Grace is all around us; it is a free gift from a loving God, and it is offered to everyone. It is God communicating God's own self to us. And we hear this divine self-communication through everyday events and words. When we pause to hear this Word, we find that it is present in the very ordinary experience of life. But, beset with sin, which is also part and parcel of living in the world, and which prevents us from completely hearing the Word, we struggle to hear: The shouting of our hearts can be so loud!

And, since we cannot always hear, it is sometimes very difficult for us to be who we are created to be. But we live with the power of grace as the engine that hums deep within us, giving us more than enough energy to go on, to become our true selves. If anything is clear here, it is that this movement of grace in our lives and in the life of the church, does not wait to be scheduled in a parish bulletin or a sacramental program. (It might be sustained by the parish with its schedule of sacraments, but that same parish could also be an obstacle to grace.)

Prayer comes to us in this same way. Prayer is not an ideal which is outside of us, something to be achieved. It is an integral part of being human: We are naturally oriented to prayer. Our awareness of ourselves, others, the earth, and God comes from our ability to reflect and pray. We have an inborn hunger for God.

My question is this: If prayer is so fundamental to being human, why do we make it seem so difficult? Why do we make it such a far-off goal? Why do we complicate it with so much falderal?

As we said earlier, we sometimes summon God in prayer, as though God were not already here. "Come holy spirit..." we say. "Our Father in Heaven..." "Come, Lord Jesus, come..." The God of these prayers must be somewhere else or we would not have to call him or her, would we? The church buildings, too, reach their spires into the skies, suggesting that God is somewhere out there. But we know that isn't true. The words are given to Jesus, himself, that the kingdom of heaven is within us. "Do not go looking here or there," the text says.

We do not need to call God to come to us from somewhere outside of us. Rather, we need to ask for the grace of perception, of spiritual insight, so that we would be able to see that we are fundamentally oriented and already journeying toward this Holy Mystery which we have named "God."

▪ THE PRAYER OF GRACE ▪

The prayer of grace, then, is not a climbing out of ourselves to God; it is not a leaving of ourselves behind in order to move into God, but rather it is a falling back to our very Center. The prayer of grace does not make us more divine: It makes us more human.

More human? Yes. More human. Remember that, in his forty days of desert time, Jesus was not tempted to act like a human. He was tempted there to forsake his humanity and act like God: 'Turn these stones into bread." "Throw yourself down and let the angels bear you." He was tempted to abandon the truth that he'd come to reveal, namely, that being fully and authentically human actualizes the potential planted within us at creation.

Being human, after all, is how we were created. Remember the text which says that Jesus did not deem equality with God something to be grasped at but rather that he became human, being born one of us. And it was when he accepted that which perhaps makes us most human—death—that God highly exalted him. We should never pray, therefore, to be less human. We should pray, instead, to be made more human, more fully who we are created to be.

It seems more comforting to pray to God in all God's glory! It seems to lift us out of the mundane, out of the ordinary, out of the everydayness of life. But, like it or not, God chose to make the earth a place of glory. This is how God chose to express God's self. This is it; this is all there is. And this is plenty!

So we will not find God by escaping the earth. Rather than looking outside of ourselves or our world, we need to look within to find what we want. The heart of the Lord can be discovered and visited only through our own hearts. In prayer, we gather up all the pieces of our often-fragmented existence and we hold them consciously in order to gain a still point, a focus: the heart. This is the place where God dwells. "The kingdom is not here or there: No, the kingdom is within you."

Jesus' own center, his still point, his own heart, was completely in the one he called Father, which was why he could so easily see God. Our heart must also rest in the one we know as Father or Mother, as Creator, as Force of Life.

We need to pray the prayer of grace: a prayer of acceptance and conversion. Basil Pennington has helped us to see that what is needed for us to pray in this way are three things only: a desire to be with God, a lonely place, and a quiet heart.

We can be very uncomfortable with silence, though, and we sometimes keep an "interior noise" going, stimulated by exterior events, all of which prevent us from hearing the stirrings of our hearts. We are unwilling to Pause, unwilling to listen, but, until we do, we will not discover the Heart of the Lord. Why do we fear prayer? We fear it because we know that, if we really ever moved to our Center, if we really ever encountered the Lord there, we would also, simultaneously, encounter ourselves. We fear that we will find ourselves somehow ugly, unlovable, incapable. We have so accepted the so-called ideal person presented in modern times in advertising and the media, that we cannot bear to see our own real selves, full of scars, pimples, fears, and, in general, full of humanness. Like the couple in the story of the Garden at creation, we don't want to be just human; we think it would be better to be God. But this is the point: It's great to be human! Even God is fully human. This is the place where we live. There is no other place than this for us. Being fully human is our mission, our goal, our created purpose.

What fools we are! If we would only allow the silence to well up around us, we would discover God there, blessing us for who we are, not scolding us for failing to be divine!

We would find at our center, present there as promised, only beauty, not ugliness. We would find only goodness, not evil. And we would find only light, never darkness. For, if we could summon the courage to make that journey of grace, we would find God there, living in our Hearts.

But, you protest, and rightly so, "How can we hear God? How does God answer us in prayer?" A fair question. God, Rahner has pointed out (*Christian at the Crossroad*, trans by V. Green (New York: Crossroad, 1975), pp. 62-69), does not speak many "words" to us. Rather, God speaks a single Word in the one who prays. That Word, filled with grace and truth, that divine Word, is nothing less than the life of the one who prays. That life, seen now from the point of view of God, is a life ever more oriented to Mystery, ever more open to the Holy, ever more fully human. God's answer to our prayer is our very life. We are revealed to ourselves, empowered to live, and readied for work.

The Word God speaks to us in prayer is our own very selves. But in order to hear this Word, we must silence ourselves, our noisy hearts, and make room there for this Word to echo. Silence of the heart will lead us to this Mystery. (The word "mystery" comes from a Greek word meaning "to keep silence.") But, because this silencing of our hearts requires a death-to-self, which is frightening for us, which appears lonely for us, and which will inevitably lead us to uncertain places, that Word spoken by God also has the power to cause us to take flight and to take refuge in the safer realm of materialism or other forms of escape. But when we pray the prayer of grace, and we resist this urge to take flight, we can allow the Word, spoken in silence by God who loves us, to take deep root in us.

Then we can contemplate the loveliness of this most Holy Mystery, and our journey inward will bring us to rest. "Be still and know that I am God."

Abraham Heschel, a great Jewish theologian, has called prayer an "ontological necessity," which is to say, an "inborn hunger for God." He echoes the teachings of Christ in so doing, and leads us home with these words. And our own catechism actually begins with this very thought, that we humans experience hunger, a hunger to be with God. If that is true, if there is such an inborn hunger, then can prayer really be far away from us? Can the Abba Father of Jesus still be a distant god?

THE GOD REVEALED BY JESUS

Jesus' Abba was not like other gods, not like the gods of the ancients, not a distant being, not a moody judge, not an absent ruler. Jesus' Abba was near, always at his side, the source of love, the truth, the destiny of his life. Abba is a mystery, of that there is little question. But the mystery is one of depth, not of confusion.

The mystery of Abba is like the depth of love, the brilliance of light, the profundity of truth. It is not that we cannot understand but rather that there is so much to know, that we can never plumb it all. In a sense, Abba is so near, so much an integral part of being human that we cannot escape God's love. There is nowhere to hide, as the Scriptures tell us, nowhere we could not be found.

There are no moods in Jesus' Abba, none at all. God is sure, steady, relentless in loving us. The power of Jesus' Abba is not to overpower others, lord it over them...." It's the power of commitment, solidarity, forgiveness, and peace. It's a power that transforms but it does so from within our souls, within our communities. This powerful, loving experience of God, this Abba experience, is one that even sinners have available to them. There is no revenge in the God of Jesus, no retaliation, no desire for repayment.

In short, Jesus illumines for us his Abba, his source and his destiny. We ourselves now find that this illumination continues in Christ, the risen One. We find illumined in our lives a depth of mystery, a power of love, a revelation of truth, a movement toward wholeness, oneness, holiness. We are in communion with God, intimate, deep communion. And this communion, this intense moment of God's presence, this experience of Abba is *prayer*.

—————— ● 9 ● ——————

Teaching Grace
TO OTHERS

*Once we have become convinced
that noticing and living with grace
is important to us,
we will want to share that
with others.*

We're going to talk about that next by sharing one of the great stories of the Christian Scriptures. This is the story of Philip, one of the people called by Jesus. Now, I know that Jesus invited quite a few people to follow him. We want to take a minute now to step back and consider how he did this calling.

The Gospels are not a biographical account of the life of Jesus. There are, in fact, many details about the life of Jesus that have been lost to history. We aren't sure where or what he did on a day-to-day basis. Those personal facts really aren't important. At least, they weren't to the early followers of Jesus who wrote the stories down. But there are some things that we can surely surmise about his life and his way of being with others. We take these surmisings from the whole gospel: We read the text and we can say, based on what was finally included, that Jesus was this sort of person or that sort. We are fully able to draw some conclusions there about what was behind the stories that were written down. What was behind them, their context, is really very important because it helps us know what the writers meant to say.

For example, we probably wouldn't conclude, from what is written there, that Jesus was given to much violence. There just isn't anything in the text to support that. Nor would we say that he was insensitive to others. He seemed, in fact, to be very sensitive: weeping, caring, noticing. We could certainly conclude, it seems to me, from what we see in the text, that Jesus had a very inclusive approach to his friendships as well as to the Kingdom of God.

Furthermore, many of the stories that we have about Jesus are summaries of much more that must have gone on. I mean, the entire text of the gospels can be read in less than a few hours but it summarizes many years in the life of a very active man and his friends and family. It is helpful for us, within limits, to consider what each story is

meant to tell us by considering what the story summarizes in the life of Jesus and the men and women who were
with him. For example, Jesus heals someone. On the face
of it, that seems pretty simple. But is it?

Those healing stories can tell us a great deal about
Jesus and his friends. They are not the stories of a first-
century magician walking down country roads zapping
people with healing, waving his hand like a wand and stir-
ring up the evil spirits of the day.

No. They are much richer than that. They summarize a
relationship between Jesus and the women and men who
were healed.

A relationship: The gospel is about relationships, healed
and healing relationships. Who knows what must have
gone on between Jesus and those seeking healing in his
presence? Who can guess the depth of compassion and
care that he must have shown to them? Time and again,
when everyone else had given up on someone, or con-
demned them, Jesus was the one brave enough and big
enough to stay with them and offer them friendship. First
it was this woman, then that man. Then he would take on
the crowd in defense of a so-called public sinner. Soon he
would turn up here healing this one, then he would show
up there healing that one. The only ones he did not bother
to defend were the self-righteous. He must have figured
that they and their judgmental attitudes could defend
themselves.

Who would Jesus defend today? Wouldn't he stand
with those caught in the nightmare of divorce? Healing
relationships was one of his specialties. Would he not be

in solidarity with those living according to their sexual orientations? Would he not confront those who continue to batter and brutalize women, whether physically or economically? And would he not continue to call the religious self-righteous, especially those who have taken it on themselves to condemn others, to account?

There are others, many others, whom Jesus would likely defend or confront today. We live in a much more complex world, much more militarized, much more psychologized, much more mobile, rapid, and linked. It is much more complex, but Jesus would sort it out, as he did the world of the first century, and hold it accountable to his central question: Does this build or destroy relationships? Is this unilateral, or is it relational? Sorting it out this way is what we must do.

Our God is a God of love, a God of commitment, of care for us, of unconditionality, of relationship with us. What happened in the Genesis story about the Garden and the people who lived there is a story about relationships, too. But in the Garden, our relationships were not healed, they were ruptured. There the people, the man and the woman, were ruptured from each other as much as they were from God.

The story tells us that they had had nothing to hide, but still there was shame. They had only each other but now there were secrets between them. The one mind and one heart that they had felt and lived with were now no longer one, they were divided, ruptured, ruined, and destroyed.

This is our story, you see, told about someone else. The story of Genesis is true, literally true, but it is true about us, not about them. That's the point of the writer.

It is never very helpful for us to use a single line of the Scriptures to try to prove this point or that. Yet certain people frequently do this. They want to show that this act or that one is sinful, as though Jesus would have said so if he were here. Or else they want to take certain specific lines of the Gospels as literal, in order to serve their purpose, while they willy-nilly ignore others. This is a-la-carte scriptural literalism and it doesn't fly very well. Rather, we should try to look at the whole gospel to understand what Jesus would teach in our day.

Story after story in the gospels remind us that Jesus was a person of love. His own words, and the words attributed to him later by those who knew him, are filled with appeals to love others. So, when the gospels tell us that someone who encountered Jesus was healed, they are summarizing a friendship. They're summarizing a way that Jesus related to this person, a way he had of loving them and of being loved by them.

Jesus meant not only to teach us of God's love but also to show us that we are capable of that depth of love, too. So we must conclude that, while Jesus loved and healed in his day, he was also loved by others, and was healed by them as well. In short, the healing and loving of Jesus and his friends was a two-way street. Don't forget that Jesus was fully human and as much in need of love as we are!

JESUS AND HIS FRIEND PHILIP

Well, getting back to Philip, the same is true there. When Jesus called Philip, he didn't just walk by him, glance sideways at him, and say, "Follow me." Heavens no. The call of Philip must have been the culmination of a long, maybe lifelong friendship, or at least of a steady relationship that allowed Philip to see Jesus plainly and Jesus to see Philip plainly.

"I call you friends," Jesus once told his closest followers, "because I have revealed myself entirely to you." Does that sound like something that could happen in a mere moment?

With Peter, James, and John, the fishermen, it may have been even more. Jesus loved the sea. In some of the gospel accounts we find story after story of him crossing over the lake, teaching from a boat, spending time on the beach. As an adult, Jesus probably lived in Capernaum which is a small town located on the Sea of Galilee. He may have lived just up the street from the beach, and he was probably a merchant there. We would guess that his trade may have been woodworking since we understand that his folks were in that business. But try not to think of him as God living on your block. Think of him as just another person living there, because that is just what he was.

So there he lived, and we know that he loved the beach front so we can easily surmise that he would have spent quite a bit of time down there, watching the fishermen work, watching the boats come and go, keeping an eye on the weather a bit, and getting to know the workers. They were probably his closest friends, these guys. They were his buddies. They sort of grew up together, got to know each other, got to trust each other, and got to love each other.

There is a kind of unplanned friendship that just sneaks up on you. You see these people every day, or very frequently, and then one day you suddenly realize that you really do love them. You realize that this is the kind of friend about whom you say, "He's really a great friend; there's something really special about him!" Or, "She's the best friend anyone could ask for!" That probably pretty well describes Jesus and these folks. What they did together was they related together: They talked, explored the truth in their lives, exposed the guilt, and learned to love. It was for all of them, including Jesus, a powerful, irresistible, love: a deep, profound love, a falling in love, a being in love, a friendship. It began on this beach, and later, it would take a dramatic turn on this same beach at a breakfast fish-fry that changed the world.

Jesus and these people did eventually make a more formal pact to be together, but the agreement was mutual: we know this from the way God has acted in the whole story of salvation. Covenants are never one-way deals. It was mutual: Jesus promised to remain with them, and they promised to remain with Jesus.

So when Jesus called these guys or any of the other men or women who were in his company, he called them in the context of love. He called them to himself and to each other, and they also called him! They called him to themselves. And in this mutuality they all found peace, comfort, strength, wholeness, and holiness.

How do we know that Jesus and the men and women who joined him were such good friends? We know because we have read some of the speeches that Jesus made about life and love and we have read some of the prayers that he prayed.

All of them, the speeches and the prayers, all point to one thing: The central point of the gospel is Love, God's and ours. Does it seem reasonable, then, that Jesus, who proclaimed this message, would have been someone in love himself? Does it seem reasonable, too, that the ones called to be with him would have been in love with him and he with them?

This has all been an introduction to our thoughts about teaching grace. It has been an introduction but, in a way, it has also been the whole story about teaching grace to others. In a word, you don't teach grace to others. Grace can only be shared, only shared in love, in the context of a loving friendship. We don't like to hear this because we know how impractical it is.

We live in a world of efficiency. Numbers mean everything. We are in the habit of mass-producing Christians. We have huge confirmation classes and gigantic first communion classes. We make sure everyone gets there, everyone: ready or not. So this business of sharing grace through love is very impractical indeed. It takes a lot of time to love. And it certainly would tend to defeat the notion that a single person could ever be pastor to the very large parishes we see in the church today around the world.

But have you ever wondered about this: If Jesus had such great power to heal, why didn't he just zap the whole world before he died and make it all well? Why did he deal with so few people during his lifetime? I mean, it seems that he really had a chance and he blew it.

But did he? We've been looking at his life here from the point of view of grace and we've found that he healed, loved, cried, cared, lived, and died only in relationship to others. He lived out a model for us. He didn't just "zap" the world because he knew he had to love the world. You don't love someone by zapping them, whether with a sacrament, a blessing, or your leadership.

We can love one another into deeper faith and greater intimacy with Christ. But to do this, we must break down the large parishes and create smaller communities. These might take many forms, including households where people naturally gather as family and hangers-on. And they might be intentional, organized small communities with a program and plan of action. The genesis of whole community catechesis and lifelong faith formation have their roots in this profound theology.

God is acting in our lives and world, but we do not create God's activity. Grace is discovered from the inside out, rather than from the outside in. People become aware of their experience of God in relationship with others. When this happens, there is the chance that they can also become aware of grace, the hand of God in that. But we don't ourselves create the moment of grace.

So, while we cannot create grace, or dispense it, we can help each other be aware of it in our midst. When we want to teach about grace, we tend to start by talking about God. But really, we would be better off if we began by talking about ourselves: our experiences, our failures, our loves, our hearts. Remember what we said earlier here, that grace is a divine gift, the power which helps us become all that we are created to be. Its purpose is not to make us equal with God. Jesus himself did not deem equality with God something to be grasped at. Rather, he accepted his full humanity and became, without anything lacking, the person he was created to be. In that sense, Jesus was full of grace and power.

Our first assumption, then, if we are to teach grace to another person, is that God is already active in that person's life. The most we can do is to make that person aware of that. And more, God is present there offering peace, life, breath, and future to that person. Paul gives us insight into this in the early part of Colossians where he gives a summary of his view of who Christ is: "Christ is the energy that holds the universe together."

When we live, empowered by the Risen Christ, then everything holds together, and without Christ we can do nothing. So we must understand that we do not make God present; God is present. Period. The most we can do is to make this presence known. And taking our example from Jesus himself, that can be done only in the context of friendship and love. For all of us, young and old, the only real way to recognize and accept grace is to be formed in it. Being formed will happen over time, time of personal prayer, small group sharing, community-wide celebrations, study of Scripture, theological reflection, and spiritual friendship.

We badly need formation programs for all the adults of the church, a similar kind of formation that members of religious communities have had since earlier in this century. We really do not learn grace as much as we are formed in it. But what we need first is a willingness to Pause in our busyness, Pause to reflect on what is happening in our lives and our days. Without this willingness to Pause, all the formation programs in the world will not help us recognize God's hand in our lives. We must learn to take the time and the quieting of our hearts that will make this Holy Pause possible for us.

If we have become aware in these times of Pausing of the Holy One in our midst; If we have become filled with awareness of grace within us and around us, then teaching grace to others will not be difficult: Others will be with us and come away knowing that they have found in us what they seek for themselves.

10

Dancing
WITH GRACE

We conclude this study with a
poetic reflection.
We are radically accepted by God.
Put on your shoes. Let's dance!

Have you ever watched pairs of birds dancing
    in the sky?
  They touch, circle, return, and touch again.
  Then they seem to disappear but just as quickly
    reappear,
    still dancing together.

Sometimes it seems to be a chase,
   sometimes a waltz,
   sometimes a race.
It appears playful,
   gentle,
   loving.

It would not occur to me that one of the birds
    would fly away
and never return to the dance!
They are together, and alone there would be no dance,
   no poetry,
   no birdly bliss.

In the end, our lives are a dance like that,
   a dance with God's grace.
There is no corner on the market of grace.
   In fact, there is no market.

Grace is elusive,
   poetic,
   awesome,
   uncontained.
It's a dance of love and life,
   a circling around and coming back,
   a moving in harmony
   and a race into the horizon.
     We touch it, like a kiss,
     but we never own it.
We never own it, period.

The moment we try to corner grace,
    control it,
    sell it,
    market it to others:
        Poof! It's gone!
It evades our grasp and yet it is so close at hand.

What is needed in order to have grace is
        maddeningly simple:
    We merely let go of our own controls,
    we die to ourselves in love
        and lo! grace appears to sustain us.
We let down our defenses, relax, take a step back, and
    follow the Call.

When we are attuned to Christ,
    we know this is true.
There is a choreography in life that we discover
    as we learn to trust,
    as we move beyond obstacles,
    as we discover grace.
It's vibrant, on-going, evolving, like the earth itself.
It unfolds before our very eyes
    as doors open
    and people enter
    and our hearts fill.
And then it seems to disappear,
    hidden behind our fears,
    invisible on the dark side.

For a moment,
    a great shining moment,
    we hear God's voice and we hang on with
        everything we've got
      to the truth of that.
But then again it seems to pass away and we stand,
    intently listening in silence,
    wondering where and when and how we heard it.
There seems to be no music now,
    no uptake,
    no cadence.
But the rhythm of the dance continues
      beneath the surface
    and soon it reappears.

Sometimes the dance is Zorba on the beach,
    wild!
    crazy!
    vigorous!
Sometimes it's two people dancing cheek-to-cheek
    in life and love.
Other times the dance is a circle,
    women and men joined arm in arm,
    dancing life into each other
    drawing the energy of the earth,
      sharing solidarity
      or Eucharist.

For our part, we need these things to learn this dance
     of life,
  this dance of grace:
     to hear the inner music,
     to let it move us,
     and to follow its rhythms.
Let the dance begin!

MY PERSONAL NOTES

MY PERSONAL NOTES

◼ OF RELATED INTEREST ◼

The Breath of the Soul
Reflections on Prayer
JOAN CHITTISTER

This simple book from a great spiritual giant offers advice for making prayer more authentic and a profound part of one's life. Great spiritual reading for all who long for God—and prayer—to be at the core of their lives.

120 pages | $12.95 | 95-747-7 | Hardcover

Forgiveness
One Step at a Time
JOSEPH F. SICA

As Christians we are challenged to embrace forgiveness. Here Fr. Joe offers ten steps to help readers take forgiveness seriously, and he has choreographed them beautifully to connect with Jesus' gospel teachings.

152 pages | $12.95 | 95-762-0

God's Enduring Presence
Strength for the Spiritual Journey
JOYCE RUPP

These beautiful reflections are filled with hope and abiding faith in God's presence and are intended to help readers discover that "deeper place" within with the spiritual assurance that God is always with them.

136 pages | $12.95 | 95-720-0

Catholic Customs & Traditions
A Popular Guide
GREG DUES

For 20 years now, this has been a bestseller—and it's still going strong. Author Greg Dues traces the vast riches of the traditions, customs, and ritual practices that make up the Roman Catholic experience.

224 pages | $19.95 | 95-771-2 | Hardcover

The Catholic Way to Pray
An Essential Guide for Adults
KATHLEEN GLAVICH, SND

Here Catholics will find ALL the information and inspiration they need to jumpstart their prayer lives. Highly recommended for catechists, parish ministers, and RCIA teams—and a great gift book for any adult Catholic.

120 pages | $9.95 | 95-755-2

Habits of the Soul
Learning to Live on Purpose
LINDA PERRONE ROONEY

This engaging resource taps into the best of Catholic tradition when it comes to living a virtuous—and thus fulfilled—life. Readers can use this day by day for forty days as a prayerful and reflective spiritual retreat.

160 pages | $14.95 | 95-554-X

TO ORDER
visit **www.23rdpublications.com**
or call **1-800-321-0411**